AF248918

HOWELL

Beginner's guide to

German Shepherds

David Alderton M.A.

Editor
Dennis Kelsey-Wood

HOWELL BOOK HOUSE Inc.
230 Park Avenue
New York, N.Y. 10169

Library of Congress Cataloging-in-Publication Data

Alderton, David, 1956-
  Howell beginner's guide to German Shepherds.

  Bibliography: p. 47
  Summary: Discusses the history and the general characteristics of the German shepherd and gives information
on selecting, training, feeding, housing, breeding, and
other aspects of caring for this breed of dog.
  1. German shepherd dogs—Juvenile literature.
[1. German shepherd dogs. 2. Dogs] I. Kelsey-Wood,
Dennis. II. Title. III. Title: Beginner's guide to
German Shepherds.
SF429.G37A43 1985   636.7'3   85-18176
ISBN 0-87605-924-8

Printed in Hong Kong through Bookbuilders Ltd

Photographs © Panther Photographic International 1983

Line illustrations by Alethea Saville and © Colorbank 1983

Contents

1. History of the Breed

The German Shepherd Dog is probably the most well known breed of dog in the world. Its natural beauty, intelligence and loyalty have endeared it to owners in almost every country to the point where it has become the most popular household dog. It excels at everything it does and can be seen as a guard dog, tracker, rescue dog, drug detector and guide for the blind. Its original role, however, was first and foremost that of a sheepdog, a role at which it is a superb master to this day. Such is the adaptability of the German Shepherd that it works as well in sub-zero temperatures as it does in the tropics.

Origins

Reference to the numerous books that have been devoted to the German Shepherd over the years shows that many authors claim great antiquity for the breed which is variously credited as having its origins 'in Egypt at the time of the Pharaohs', 'during the Bronze Age' or other similar and equally unsubstantiated theories. The fact is, that like most other breeds, the ancestry of the German Shepherd is quite recent; certainly no-one could define it as a breed as such, much earlier than about 120 years ago and, even then, it would be very doubtful.

Natural beauty, loyalty and intelligence are characteristics of the German Shepherd.

Any further back than this, and one is left with nothing more than paintings, sketches, statues and other artefacts which are purported to be evidence of its early beginnings, but which could, in truth, equally be applicable to dozens of other present day breeds of dog. The further fact that sheepdogs were the property of poor farmers who kept no records of matings or pedigrees is an indication that the claims mentioned are at best misleading and at worst ridiculous. With the formation of societies devoted towards a common goal, came the recording of dogs and their lineage and to their improvement on the basis of a written standard of excellence; without these factors there would be no such breed as the German Shepherd as we now know it.

In order to get a clearer picture of the origin and development of this breed and to deal with the question of 'wolf blood' (that has always haunted the German Shepherd), one needs to look no further back than the 16th century. At that time, throughout Europe, there was a multifarious array of sheepdogs which had the dual role of guard and shepherd. They protected against both thieves and wild beasts of which the wolf was the prime predator. Such dogs came in all manner of shapes and sizes, some were long-coated, some were short-coated and others wire-haired. They were bred and mated on the basis of their reputations as working dogs rather than on how they looked; as breeding was a somewhat localized arrangement, the result was that, at most, one could establish regional 'types'.

There is no doubt that, during this period, wolf blood was introduced in order to give strength and intelligence to existing stock; it is a practice still used in polar regions in order to improve eskimo husky breeds. This practice was to remain in use until the wolf had largely been exterminated over much of Europe.

By the early 19th century very little change had taken place except insofar as the need for guarding, whilst still there, was being superseded by the more highly-developed shepherding skills. Type still reflected the terrain in which dogs had to work, be it in mountainous country, flat lands, warmer or colder regions. By today's standards breeding was still random, with details of lineage by word of mouth rather than by written documentation. Thus it can be seen that there were in Germany, at this time, many types of shepherding dogs but no German Shepherd as such. Those types will have figured in the development of other breeds such as the Groenendael, Laekenois, Malinois, Tervuren and various other breeds now established in the many European countries where shepherd dogs then abounded.

Establishment of the Breed

In 1899 the *Verein für Deutsche Schäferhunde* (or SV as it is known) was formed and with this society came the proper organization that marks the true beginnings of the dog as a breed. The second president of the SV was a Capt. von Stephanitz, who is regarded as the father of the breed; under his guidance the SV turned what was initially a motley collection of types into a recognized breed. From a membership of just thirty-one people in 1899, the ranks swelled to forty-five thousand in the first twenty-three years. Today, the membership stands at in excess of one hundred and forty thousand making it the largest animal society in the world devoted to a single species.

Although the effective introduction of wolf blood would not have been possible after the turn of the twentieth century (when dogs of unknown pedigree could not be registered with the SV) this still left a question mark over a number of dogs already registered and, in particular, *Mores Plieningen* (the one hundred and fifty-ninth registered animal) a bitch to whom probably every living German Shepherd can today be traced. Having said this, it must also be pointed out that over thirty generations have passed since then and, to quote the eminent geneticist, Dr M. B. Willis (1976), in his famous tome on the breed 'The influence of this cross cannot be more than negligible and should be a matter of total indifference to all'.

The German Shepherd was quickly found to be adaptable and the German army made good use of this fact during the First World War. The breed was first imported into the USA in 1906 in the form of *Mira von Offingen* and a few were also imported into the UK prior to 1914, though not in sufficient numbers for them to be given a separate register. The war enabled British officers to see them first hand, and many were taken back to the UK where the breed soon flourished. The story is the same the world over – wherever the breed was seen it flourished – often in spite of continual attacks from the Press who questioned its reliability as a household pet.

The problem stemmed from the fact that, with the rapid growth of popularity of the breed following the success of such movie stars as *Strongheart* and *Rin-Tin-Tin*, unscrupulous dealers concentrated on quantity rather than quality and many dogs found their way into homes to which they were totally unsuited, and with disastrous results. However, the breed rose above all this 'scare-mongery' and, by continual excellent service to man coupled with thoughtful breeding by dedicated devotees, has maintained its position as the world's best canine all-rounder.

The UK Name Controversy

Whilst most countries, sensibly, adopted a straight translation of the German name for the breed, the UK did not because it was felt that, following the 1914–18 war, this would not endear it to the British public; it was, therefore, decided to name the dog after the German-Franco area of Alsace-Lorraine. Thus the name used was Alsatian, to which Wolf-dog was added. This latter term was quickly dropped as it did nothing to help the breed's image and, in 1936, the English Kennel Club gave the name of Alsatian (German Shepherd Dog) to the breed. Following numerous campaigns by dedicated breeders, the KC finally gave way to sense and, in 1977, officially employed German Shepherd Dog as the name for the breed.

2. The Selection and Care of a Puppy

It should be stated clearly from the outset that not all prospective dog-owners are suitable for German Shepherd Dogs, and vice-versa. Having a dog of any kind should be viewed as a two-way interaction, rather than just from the owner's standpoint. In some cases, for example, a German Shepherd Dog is acquired merely to form an extension of the owner's apparently aggressive nature, and this invariably results in subsequent problems. In fact, the breed itself has a very sensitive nature which, in turn, makes it very responsive to its owner.

Some characteristics of German Shepherds, such as their size, which appeal to certain people will deter others from selecting a dog of this breed. Although a puppy usually appears cuddly, it will normally grow up into a large, active dog which requires regular, daily exercise. The various aspects of ownership, such as the space available and the costs involved, must be considered properly before acquiring a dog. A puppy, in particular, will require large amounts of time spent with it, and should never be acquired if the house is likely to be empty for most of the day or night.

You can learn a great deal by attending a dog show before purchasing a puppy.

Obtaining a Puppy

There are many ways to locate a suitable puppy and many desirable places to find one. Know what you want before you start. Contact with Shepherd breeders can often be made through a local veterinary surgeon, or the columns of the dog magazines and sometimes even the local Press. By going to visit a number fo kennels (the more the better) you have the opportunity to see not only the puppies but also at least one of the parents, together with other stock bred by that breeder. Visiting shows is another means of contact and particularly to be recommended if one is hoping to obtain a puppy for later exhibition. It gives an opportunity of seeing at first hand what type of dog is required by judges, and the procedure adopted at such events.

Choosing a Puppy

It is much easier to select a puppy for a pet, rather than as a potential show champion. Nevertheless, there are several fundamental points which should be observed when considering any puppy. By the age of about eight weeks, the young dog should be fully weaned, and able to make the transition to life in a new home with the minimum of problems. An older dog, having lived in a kennel all its life, is more likely to be nervous, and harder to house-train.

Before handling a puppy, the owner's permission should be requested, and then, supporting the rear end firmly with a hand or arm, the puppy can be examined more closely. A healthy youngster will be quite plump, with an adequate covering of puppy fat, but a distinct pot-bellied appearance is a sign of poor health, caused perhaps by intestinal worms.

There should be no abnormal swelling around the umbilicus, or navel, as this could prove to be a hernia which may require later surgical treatment. The underparts should also be examined for any spots or signs of redness, which could be a cause for concern.

The dew claws should have been removed from the inner surfaces of the hind legs when the litter was about four days old. Later removal is possible, but is a much more serious matter. These claws are in fact vestigial, and are liable to be a problem, becoming overgrown or caught up, later in the dog's life. The front dew claws should not be removed from a German Shepherd that is intended for exhibition purposes. In fact, not all dogs possess a full complement of dew claws.

When examining the limbs, they must not show any signs of bowing, which may be indicative of rickets. It is, however, quite normal for the knee joints of a young German Shepherd puppy to appear relatively large, as may its feet. The claws should all be black.

With this breed, the ears may not become erect until six months of age or even later, while with some this is never achieved. Individuals with relatively large, heavy ears are more likely to suffer this fault, so those which show signs of lifting their ears early are generally to be preferred. The incidence of ear infections is likely to somewhat higher in flat-eared dogs.

The jaws of the mouth should meet well, with neither one being longer than the other, as this is a serious fault. The eye color is a variable characteristic, ranging from yellow to dark brown. Yellow eyes are penalized in show circles, although the color is otherwise allowed to correspond to the surrounding fur. The eyes are an important feature because they contribute a great deal to the facial expression of the dog. The coat is a useful indicator of health; it should be bright and full of luster.

It is always worth noting how the puppy reacts when being placed back on the ground. It should appear lively and even playful. The carriage of the tail is significant, because a nervous dog keeps its tail between its legs, and is harder to settle successfully.

Coat Color and Texture

The coat of a German Shepherd Dog should ideally consist of a coarse outer layer of guard hairs which protect the denser undercoat. Long-coated specimens are still seen although these are not favored in the showring. Very short-coated dogs are equally undesirable, having an ugly appearance, though they are technically acceptable. The correct coat will be of medium length but, as this is a relative term, prospective owners are advised to see as many specimens as possible in order to appreciate that which is most desirable.

Coat colors may be broadly divided into five groups, these being as follows:

1. *White:* This may range from pure white to a very dirty, almost yellow, off-white. It is not recommended and is outlawed by the breed standard for exhibition purposes.
2. *Sables:* These range from light fawns to deep golds and from pale silvers to very dark grays or agoutis. Not as popular as they once were, they can nevertheless be very striking and attractive. Sables mated with Sables can produce Sables, Saddle-marked, Bi-colored and Blacks.
3. *Saddle-marked:* Such dogs have a black saddle with either silver/gray or tan/gold on the rest of the body.
4. *Bi-colored:* These dogs are predominantly black with tan markings on the legs, chest, eyebrows and, sometimes, muzzle. *Saddle-marked* and *Bi-colored* are treated as separate by most breeders but, in fact, both are variations of the *Black and Tan* coloration. Obvious examples are easy to recognize but the difference between the two can be very difficult to distinguish.
5. *Black:* These are totally black all over. Contrary to popular belief, all black in the German Shepherd is not dominant to other colors.
Muzzles: The muzzle of dogs found in (2) and (3) may be of the same color

as the surrounding fur or it may be black – the latter being the more popular.

When selecting a puppy it can be very difficult to assess what the adult color will look like but, as the light areas will spread, those requiring dogs for exhibition should choose one of the darker members of the litter.

Dog or Bitch?

The sex of the puppy must also be considered, again from both viewpoints. Generally bitches are more tolerant of children than are dogs, but the problem of their two breeding heats each year may cause considerable trouble. They are, nevertheless, preferred as guide dogs, and a vet can advise on ways of lessening the difficulties arising from their cycle. If it is hoped to breed from the puppy later, then a bitch should be chosen. However, male dogs make excellent companions, so it is really a question of one's personal circumstances.

Paperwork

Having chosen a puppy, it is important to sort out the necessary paperwork with the breeder concerned. The pedigree shows the ancestry of the puppy extending back over four or five generations, but is not in itself a registration document. The breeder should have registered the litter with the Kennel Club within four weeks of their birth and may subsequently have named each puppy individually for the register.

If this is the case, then it will be necessary to complete a transfer form which, together with the original registration document, must be sent to the Kennel Club so that the change of ownership can be recorded. Alternatively, it is simply a matter of selecting a suitable name to accompany the registration form.

The breeder should be asked for a diet sheet, and the feeding regimen to which the puppy is accustomed. It is also useful to know whether the pup has been wormed, and which treatment has been used, if this is known. Any vaccination certificates should also be requested. The Kennel Club registration, and the pedigree may be available at the time of collection, but often there is a delay in obtaining the registration documents. It is much easier to sort out the relevant paperwork at this stage, rather than leaving it until a later date.

Taking the Puppy Home

The puppy should be moved in a snug cardboard box, lined with an old clean towel. This is the safest method, because the young dog will not be used to the unfamiliar motion of the car, and may well be sick as a result. It will, in fact, take a while for the body's senses to become accustomed to this new sensation.

On Arrival Home

Now, in a strange environment, away from his fellows, the puppy should be allowed to settle down quietly for a day or so. On arrival, it is a good idea to offer a milky drink, in which some glucose or honey has been dissolved. Goat's milk is less likely to cause diarrhoea than cow's milk, especially if the puppy is not used to the latter. The mixture should be given lukewarm, rather than hot or cold.

The feeding regimen adopted by the breeder should be adhered to, if at all possible, for the first few days, as this will help reduce the risk of digestive disturbances. For the same reason, food containers must always be washed thoroughly after each meal and a fresh bowl of water given daily.

Kennelling

While the majority of people who keep a pet German Shepherd Dog will want it to live in the home, a few prefer, for a variety of reasons, to house their dog in an outdoor kennel. Various companies produce individual kennels, or ranges, which should always be sited on well-drained land whenever possible. The shelter of the kennel must be dry and draught-proof, as well as being easy to clean. A raised bed, with suitable bedding is also recommended.

Outdoor runs can have a covering of earth or grass, although these are very difficult to keep clean. Concrete floors can be somewhat hard on the feet, but are easily washed off. Gravel provides quite good drainage, like concrete, but is much harder to clean off satisfactorily. The sides of the run should be set into the ground on blocks, to deter any dog from digging out, while the roof can be open, or wired over. This will be influenced partly by the height of the structure, which, for convenience of access, should be ideally about 1·8 metres (6 feet).

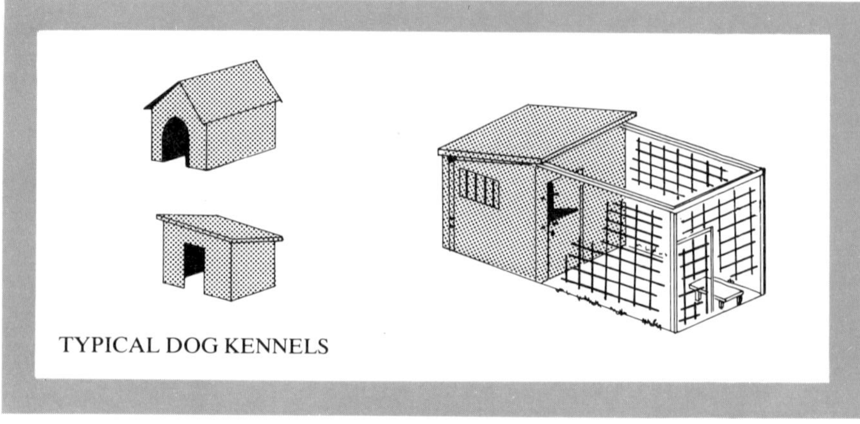

COAT COLORS AND PATTERNS IN THE GERMAN SHEPHERD DOG

Black and Tan

Black and Silver

Black

Sable

White

Agouti

Bedding

The puppy should be encouraged to recognize and use its own bed from the outset. A washable bed is to be recommended, but it may be worth deferring the decision as to the type until after the teething phase has passed. Initially a cut-down cardboard box will suffice and this can be lined with old newspapers, using some clean blanketing or sheets on top for the dog to lie on.

Veterinary Advice

A visit to a local veterinarian should be made soon after its acquisition, so that the puppy can be given a check-over and the necessary vaccinations. Until these take effect, giving satisfactory immunity, it is not advisable to take the puppy out for walks in public places such as parks, or allow close contact with other dogs. This does not mean that the youngster should be kept indoors in complete isolation, because an early period of so-called 'socialization' is important with German Shepherd Dogs. Given the run of a garden, and taken out for drives in the car ensures their natural curiosity is not inhibited, leading to subsequent nervousness.

The veterinarian will be able to advise on the use of dietary supplements, such as calcium and Vitamin D_3 preparations for good bone development. A worming program is another important consideration to be discussed with the vet, who can prescribe suitable, effective treatments for the various parasitic worm infections which a puppy may encounter. These may well differ according to the region of the world concerned, as discussed later.

Vaccinations

These usually offer protection against distemper and canine hepatitis, caused by viruses, as well as leptospirosis which results from a bacterial infection. All these diseases can prove fatal, so it is sensible to take advantage of the protection provided by vaccination. The vaccines are usually packed in a combined dose and given together, rather than as three separate injections. Side-effects are very rarely encountered, but if the puppy has been 'off-color' just beforehand, the veterinarian must be informed because the vaccination could otherwise prove harmful. A separate vaccine to protect against parvovirus, which has caused epidemics of disease in many countries recently, is also now recommended by many veterinarians, especially for younger dogs.

3. Training

German Shepherd Dogs are generally very responsive to training, as exemplified by the various police dog displays held at many outdoor events. Training in the domestic environment is not a difficult procedure, merely a question of routine, coupled with firmness and understanding on the part of the owner. Many towns have organized dog training classes which meet regularly, and serve to assist both owners and their charges with the basic procedures. The Kennel Club has laid down specific tests for Obedience Classes, marked on a points system, for those who then wish to develop their dog's natural ability to the maximum.

House Training

Contrary to what people may sometimes think, dogs are not generally dirty creatures by nature, but puppies need to be taught where they can attend to their natural functions. A puppy will soon respond to being placed outside, when it appears to want to defaecate or urinate. In the first instance, provision of a box lined with newspaper and filled with sand or a similar absorbent substance will serve as a dirt box. This must be changed as soon as possible after it has been soiled.

Feeding will usually be followed by bowel movement, and a young puppy may naturally go perhaps six times a day, and urinate even more frequently. This also often happens when the pup wakes up after a snooze.

It is pointless to scold a puppy which has not used its box. Instead, the young dog should be placed outdoors for a brief period, although it is preferable to anticipate the need before it arises. Puppies soon learn to ask to go out when necessary. At night, it is perhaps most effective to have the puppy in the bedroom, and then put the youngster outdoors directly it appears distressed. Within about a week, the pup should be able to sleep undisturbed for most of the night.

A distasteful problem which may arise, especially in the older dog originally kept in kennels, is coprophagy, when it eats its own faeces. This is sometimes regarded as the dog's attempt to keep its quarters clean, but it may also result from a dietary deficiency of Vitamin B, which should be supplemented as a precautionary measure. Such behaviour can rapidly develop into a habit, however, so temptation must be removed as soon as it emerges.

Obedience Training

The tone of voice is one of the most potent tools in the trainer's repertoire, and the puppy will soon learn to distinguish between a harsh voice and a more favorable tone. Firmness and patience, rather than force, will yield the best results. However, it is important not to confuse the young dog; for example, when the puppy is using a dirt box, praising it while walking away may result in a following trail over the carpet. A harsh scolding under such circumstances is unjustified.

Obedience training should begin early in the puppy's new life, so that a basic routine is established from the outset. If the dog is not going to be allowed on to chairs or other furniture, it is much easier and fairer, to make this clear from the beginning. The two simple commands which must be mastered initially are 'stay' and 'sit'. With guidance, these are not difficult for the dog to learn. Placing the puppy in its bed, after feeding or exercise (when it should want to sleep) and repeating 'stay' until the command is obeyed, will soon result in this order being recognized.

Teaching the puppy to sit can be carried out with the 'stay' routine. At first, it may be necessary to apply gentle pressure to the dog's hind quarters to achieve this posture. This can be repeated at every opportunity, such as before putting down a bowl of food. The puppy should be rewarded with a titbit for responding to a command, but never deprived of its food if it fails to obey, as this will only encourage thieving and other problems.

Lead training should commence early if you are not to have problems later when the puppy grows larger – and stronger.

This youngster's ears may take another few months before they are in the typical erect position.

It is essential that all dogs are on leads when being exercized on, or near, roads.

The Big Outdoors

A fully-grown German Shepherd weighing perhaps 36kg (80 pounds) will prove a distinct liability on a lead if it is not used to walking correctly. Therefore, training should begin in the garden, with sessions lasting for a maximum of ten minutes each day, even before all vaccinations have been completed.

The puppy should be walked up and down on the lead, at first preferably sandwiched between its owner and a wall or fence, so that it cannot pull away. If the youngster starts pulling ahead, the command 'heel' should be given, and the puppy encouraged to adopt the desired position using a choke chain if necessary. If the young dog starts dragging behind, a gentle pull on the lead with words of encouragement should overcome the problem. The 'sitting' routine can also be developed in conjunction with lead walking. Always remember that, no matter how well-trained, a dog should *never* be exercised off the lead near to roads as the unforeseen can always happen with, possibly, tragic results. It just is not worth the risk.

When taken out, these procedures should be repeated, in the face of other distractions such as other pedestrians and traffic. Nevertheless, a young dog must never be over-exercised, particularly at first, and regular daily walks are much better than one long marathon each week-end.

There are various other lessons which can be taught such as the retrieving and dropping of toys and other objects. All such toys given to puppies must, however, be virtually indestructible, because otherwise parts are likely to be

15

chewed off and swallowed indiscriminately. Dangerous household objects and clothing, such as cotton reels and tights, should always be kept out of reach. If such items are ingested by the puppy, severe intestinal problems may develop and require emergency surgery.

Responsible Dog Ownership

Regrettably, the population at large contains an increasing proportion of people who dislike dogs, and the dog owner has a responsibility to the community, as well as to himself and to his pet.

Consideration for Neighbors

Left alone to its own devices, the dog is likely to wander into a road, and could cause an accident for which its owner may well be held responsible. Scavenging from dustbins and other refuse sites is likely to result in digestive upsets, apart from annoying the neighbors. Sadly, today in major cities, there are packs of dogs including pedigree animals, running wild which are a constant source of nuisance. An identification disk or similar marking must always be attached to the collar, so that if the dog does stray accidentally, and is then rounded up by the authorities, or otherwise caught, tracing its owner will be a straightforward matter.

Neighbors in the immediate vicinity can be affected very easily by the acquisition of a dog, and this can generate ill-feeling if their privacy is subsequently disturbed. A dog should be taught, from the outset, that it will be left alone for short periods and must not bark and howl incessantly during this time. This is often harder to achieve with an older animal, and in really severe cases, the only way to cope with the difficulty is to obtain tranquillizers from a veterinarian.

There is a noticeable difference between this noise and a definite, purposeful warning bark, serving to alert the dog's owner to the presence of a stranger nearby. Given a suitable introduction, the dog soon becomes familiar with neighbors, and will not bark when it sees them moving about their own property. Firmness in the early period of training will be rewarded subsequently by eliminating such bad traits before they become habitual.

Sometimes it can be difficult to stop a dog straying, especially if there is a bitch on heat in the vicinity, so the provision of secure fencing around a garden will be essential. Although dogs do not climb, German Shepherds are capable of jumping to a height of 1·8 metres (6 feet) without too much difficulty, if they are sufficiently determined. Digging can also provide an exit from a garden so, at first, the dog should if possible always be accompanied into the garden or watched closely.

When being exercised in the country, dogs must always be kept on a lead while in the vicinity of livestock. This is a legal requirement in countries such as Britain, where it is included as a provision of the Wildlife and Countryside Act, 1981. Farmers have a right to shoot dogs which are upsetting, even if not actually harming, their livestock. Dog owners can also be prosecuted for not possessing licences for their pets. These are renewable annually, being obtained from Post Offices in Britain.

Consideration for the Dog

Dogs, like other animals, appreciate a routine which starts when they are introduced to the family circle. It is preferable to be firm from the beginning, and then gradually relent as desired, rather than adopt the reverse approach. It is unfair, for example, to let the sweet little pup sleep on the bed, only to decide several weeks later that it is getting too big and so should spend the night elsewhere.

Unintentional cruelty can develop into the actual loss of a pet, especially during hot weather. Dogs will rapidly become miserable and wander off from a beach, for example, while their owners are sun-bathing. If confined to a car, especially with no ventilation, they are likely to succumb from heat-stroke and die from hyperthermia. Dogs cannot sweat efficiently like humans, but lose excess heat from their bodies by panting. They do possess some sweat glands, however, located between the pads of their feet.

Many dogs find it upsetting to be taken shopping through busy areas, surrounded by people on all sides. Other human activities, such as Bonfire Night or Independence Day Celebrations can also mean misery for pets, unless they are secured indoors, away from the fireworks. Storms may have a similar effect, with the dog choosing to hide under a chair or another place where it feels secure.

Consideration for the Family

With luck, the German Shepherd Dog will be a part of the family for over a decade. It must, therefore, adapt to its environment, while both parties realize what is expected of them. A well-trained dog is a delight for all who come into contact with it. On the other hand, soiled carpets, chewed furniture and scratched doors will result from inadequate training, and lead to family tensions.

Each dog is an individual, and part of a unique environment as a member of a home. When problems do arise, there are various individuals and organizations who can be contacted for advice. Attendance at training classes is especially useful for the novice owner, while additional help can always be sought from veterinarians and from most breeders. In the majority of cases, the owner is usually partially to blame for a behavioral problem, albeit unintentionally, and will need to be guided in order to help the dog.

4. Adult Management

As the puppy grows up into an adult, its feeding requirements and habits are bound to change, depending partly on the work which it is expected to perform. In addition, an adult dog will only require half the protein intake which was needed to sustain it during its growth phase.

'Convenience' foods are now much in evidence in the pet industry, although a varied diet, including some fresh meat, is to be recommended. There are many brands of tinned food marketed worldwide, along with various dry and semi-moist products which must always be used as directed. The latter foodstuffs may prove harmful if the manufacturer's instructions are not followed, with adverse effects on the kidneys in particular.

In the case of tinned foods, some are too rich for a few individuals, so the

The GSD is a tireless runner and enjoys nothing more than a romp in the countryside.

Always a popular attraction at shows are the highly trained Police and Army dogs. Here a GSD clears a high wall.

The dog's natural fear of fire is overcome for the spectacular leap through the wall of flames.

brand may need to be changed. Nevertheless, such tins, prepared to exacting standards, generally provide an economical way of keeping a dog in good condition. Most German Shepherd Dogs will consume two 411 gm (14½ oz) tins per day, along with biscuit meal.

Fresh Meat and Bones

As a guide, an active young German Shepherd Dog will require about 1 kg (2 pounds) of meat daily, with a couple of handfuls of biscuit meal. Those brands of meal which contain yeast are most palatable. The meal itself is a major source of carbohydrate and, if the dog appears to be getting overweight, the amount of meal in the diet should be reduced.

With older dogs particularly, it is unwise to exercise them directly after a large meal, as they may develop the condition known as dilatation of the stomach, which can be further complicated by twisting, referred to as torsion. The stomach itself becomes distended and cannot empty satisfactorily. This problem can have a very sudden onset, and requires rapid veterinary attention as it can prove fatal in a matter of hours. One of the characteristic signs is abdominal pain, followed by swelling of the affected region.

An older adult dog will do well on approximately 0·75 kg (1½ pounds) of meat, supplemented with one handful of biscuit. Beef, horsemeat and liver are all commonly used in dog feeding, but again, variety, such as cheese or fish should be introduced to the diet. The food can be given in one large meal during the early evening, or divided to make two feeds. It is important, particularly in hotter climates, not to leave uneaten food where flies and other insects can gain access to it, and so cause disease.

Bones are especially useful when puppies are teething, but they will be welcomed by older dogs as well. It is vital to give only large marrow bones, which will not splinter in the mouth, and cannot be swallowed. Chicken carcasses are very dangerous in this respect.

Exercise

Apart from playing in the garden, the adult German Shepherd Dog should be given a walk of at least one mile daily, throughout the year. Many dogs also enjoy swimming and, although the condition of the coat may deteriorate as a result, the overall muscle tone of the body is likely to be improved. After getting wet, dogs usually dry off rapidly. They have two layers of hairs in their coats, and the dense inner layer is relatively water-resistant, thus acting as an insulator.

Grooming

Regular grooming is to be recommended, not only to improve the appearance of the coat but also because it will ensure that the dog is relatively used to being handled at close quarters, and so should not resent it. There are various suitable tools for grooming, but a stout brush and comb will be essential. The bristles of the brush should be reasonably firm so that they do not just slide over the surface of the hair. A metal comb is also preferable, and will serve to remove much of the loose hair. Although dogs lose hair throughout the year, the amount lost is noticeably increased when they are molting properly. Amongst other grooming accessories, a flea comb is a valuable acquisition, while a hound- or grooming-glove is also useful for giving the coat an attractive finish.

Grooming should start from the base of the neck down to the tail, then switch to the flanks and finally the legs and head. During a molt, it is worth running a hand through the coat in the opposite direction, to loosen the hair which is then removed by combing. Although bathing is not necessary on a regular weekly basis, there are times when the dog will benefit from a bath, perhaps to control fleas for example.

The directions for using medicated shampoos must be followed closely, and the preparation itself kept out of the eyes. The water used should be tepid rather than cold, and it is obviously preferable to bath the dog outside, if possible, on warm days. Subsequently, it will need to be kept in a similar temperature to dry off, after a thorough towelling. Grooming also affords the opportunity to give an overall health check. The ears can be inspected for any signs of infection, the length of the claws noted in case they need cutting, and the mouth can be opened to examine the teeth. Regular examinations of this type ensure that subsequently, either at the vet's or at home, any treatment required is much more straightforward for the person concerned to administer, and less distressing to the dog.

The Older German Shepherd Dog

One of the most obvious signs of old age is likely to be fading of the coat color, but other insidious changes, such as progressive kidney failure may also be developing. Bad breath can be the first sign that an owner notices, although this may also result from dental decay.

A veterinary check-up is highly recommended if there is any concern over the dog's health. Although no cure exists for the effects of aging, modern treatments may well serve to help an older dog to enjoy its remaining life more fully. A urine sample, collected in a clean sugar-free container, is often a useful starting-point for a veterinary investigation.

5. Breeding

Breeding German Shepherd Dogs is a fascinating, albeit time-consuming, pastime. However, thought should be given to finding homes for surplus puppies, even before the bitch is mated. For those who are especially interested in breeding their dogs, further reference should be made to some of the books devoted solely to this topic, listed in the appendices. A brief summary is given here.

Pet Dogs

Before discussing actual mating, a word of caution must be given to those who purchased dogs purely as pets. Most reputable breeders will tell would-be owners whether the dog they are considering is suitable for breeding or not. Often, dogs which might fall short of potential exhibition standard are sold off as pets – which is not to say they are not sound healthy animals, but purely that they have a failing which would be heavily penalized in a

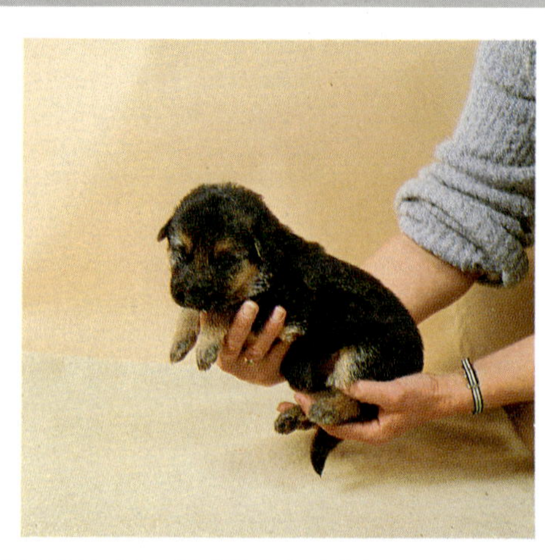

HANDLING A PUPPY

The pup must be supported with one hand whilst the other both cradles and supports the chest.

This mother is coping well with her large litter –
others may need help from you by hand feeding of
the puppies.

showring. Such dogs should never be bred from and, most certainly, not on the often heard grounds of 'I thought it would do her good'. All it does is to make available more sub-standard German Shepherds, and helps to perpetuate the very faults that the breeders are trying hard to remove.

Mating Procedure

The bitch should not be mated before her third heat, when she will be about two years old. Selecting a suitable mate for her will require a degree of honesty, to appreciate her faults, and then to look for a sire which excels in these respects. Temperament is a vital consideration, and generally nervous or unsteady dogs should not be bred from, because they are liable to produce similar offspring.

Other problems which may be inherited to a greater or lesser degree, include hip dysplasia and epilepsy. X-rays and electro-encephalograms (to pick up the abnormal brain wave pattern) respectively will confirm these conditions; so, if in doubt, veterinary advice should be sought prior to mating. Worming tablets should also be obtained for the bitch at the same time because she can infect her puppies, even before they are born, with *Toxocara canis*.

Mating is most likely to be successful from about the tenth to the fourteenth day after the first appearance of the discharge, but it can vary according to the bitch concerned. When gentle pressure on the hindquarters elicits the so-called 'standing' posture, and the vaginal discharge becomes clear, she is usually ready to accept her mate.

The process itself will probably last about twenty minutes, but it may last twice as long. The bitch's internal muscles will grip the dog's erect, swollen penis, and this is referred to as a 'tie'. Subsequently, some semen may be visible around the bitch's vulva, but this should not be a cause for concern. There are on average about 125 million spermatozoa per ml. of semen, and only one of these will be necessary to fertilize an ovum. If a second mating is planned, however, this should be carried out during the next twenty-four hours. Most established stud dogs are over two years old, but they can be tested for breeding potential from about ten months onward.

Feeding Prior to Whelping

Feeding should be carried on normally for the first few weeks of pregnancy but, subsequently, the amount of meat must be increased, by about 0·25 kg (½ pound) during both the fourth and sixth weeks. This should take the form of an extra feed at mid-day. Calcium supplements are also of increasing importance as pregnancy progresses. Milky foods such as semolina, together with fresh or evaporated milk, are important from the sixth week onwards, with the puppies being born after a gestation period of approximately nine weeks. In the latter stages, the bitch may go off her food; this is quite normal, and her appetite will soon return after she gives birth.

Whelping

Prior to whelping, the bitch's body temperature will fall, from about 38·6°C to 37·8°C (101·5°F to 100°F) or below. Preparations for the birth should be made well in advance and, although problems are not as commonly encountered in German Shepherds as other breeds, the vet should be notified, just in case professional help is needed.

Whelping Box

A whelping box, about 135 cm (4½ feet) square and 20 cm (8 inches) deep must be prepared at least a week before the puppies are due, so that the bitch can become accustomed to it. The box should only be lined with newspaper, because blanketing, for example, will become soiled, and is likely to obscure the pups, so they may be rolled on by accident. As an additional precaution against such accidents, a guard rail can be nailed around the inner surface of

24

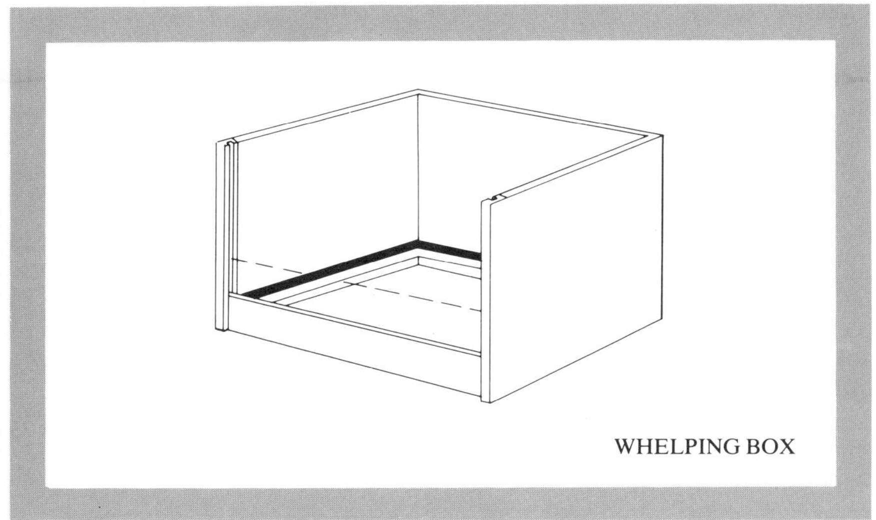

the frame about 5 cm (2 inches) wide. The room chosen for the whelping should have a temperature of about 18°C (65°F)

The Birth Itself

The bitch should be monitored, with the minimum of disturbance, to have her pups; it should always be borne in mind that she is then likely to prove very protective to her newborn offspring. Restlesness and straining are generally the most obvious signs that birth is imminent. The puppy is normally born head first, along with its water-bag, which will be ruptured immediately after birth, if it has not been burst beforehand. The umbilical cord, attaching the pup to its placenta, should also be nipped through by the mother. The afterbirth should then follow, and may be consumed by some bitches which is a normal, but not essential part, of the birth. Retention of the placenta is, however, a serious problem, so it is important to count the number that are passed.

There are various other problems that can arise both during, and immediately after, the birth process, such as puppies being presented in the 'breech' or posterior position. If in any doubt, it is preferable to seek veterinary advice rather than to interfere, as this can have serious consequences.

Rearing

It is important that the puppies should be allowed to suckle as soon as possible, to obtain the bitch's colostrum, which is a valuable source of protection against early infections. No bitch should be expected to rear more than seven puppies, and others must be transferred to another dam if at all possible, or culled as a last resort. Hand-rearing from a day old is possible, but fraught with problems, not least of which is the amount of time that will be required. It is now possible to obtain a balanced replacement feed for the bitch's milk, which is helpful.

The bitch herself should be given milky foods predominantly for the first few days, along with a continued calcium supplement. Meat can be re-introduced from about the second day, but may not be accepted immediately. Boiled white fish is popular with some individuals at this time.

There are various rearing systems used by breeders, one of which is given below, for the first month of the puppy's life.

Time	Feed for the Dam
7 a.m.	Warm milk diluted with water and whisked raw egg
8 a.m.	Semolina
11 a.m.	1 kg (2 lb) meat plus cod-liver oil capsules as directed
2 p.m.	½ pint milk
5 p.m.	0·75 kg (1½ lb) meat plus usual ration of biscuit meal
7 p.m.	Evaporated milk, with teaspoonful of honey

Obviously, however, the amount of food consumed will vary, depending on the number of puppies in the litter.

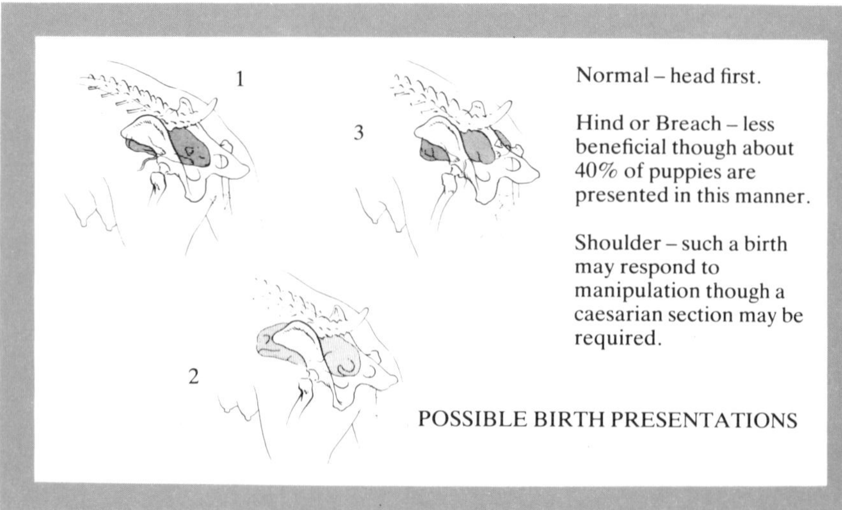

POSSIBLE BIRTH PRESENTATIONS

Weaning

This should be a gradual process which can begin once the puppies open their eyes when about two weeks old. They can be encouraged to sample meat, such as finely cut beef shin offered on the end of the finger, and then subsequently tempted to lap fluids.

From the age of about four weeks, their dam will be starting to lose interest in the pups and weaning should begin in earnest. Her food ration should be modified as shown below.

Age of Litter	Change to Dam's Diet
4 weeks	Cut out the two afternoon milk feeds gradually over several days
5–6 weeks	Reduce 11 a.m. feed by ·25 kg (½ lb)
6–7 weeks	Reduce semolina and milk to a small plateful twice daily

The bitch's milk should dry up naturally, without difficulty, as the puppies stop suckling. When the pups are about six weeks old, the dam may then start regurgitating meat for her offspring. This is natural behavior, but to compensate for it, she should be given a high-protein diet.

Select a good quality weaning food, with directions for mixing accompanying the product. Once the puppies are taking this freely, the amount of minced

The head features, both from the front and in profile, are shown in these superb photographs.

meat in the diet can be increased cautiously. A sudden change will result in digestive upsets; for the same reason, the puppies should be offered their food in relatively small quantities about five times a day, rather than as one big meal. It is important to ensure that all receive their share, and that the dam cannot steal the food. Milk, containing relatively high levels of calcium should be freely available, and supplements used as directed to ensure a healthy bone structure.

At six weeks old, the pups should be receiving four feeds daily, with alternate offerings of milk and meat. Although the actual number of meals can be reduced subsequently to three, the amount of food provided should, in fact, be increased as the puppies continue growing.

Age	Canned Food and Biscuit Meal (per feed)		'Moist' Dog Food (per feed)	Frequency
Weaning - 7 weeks	¼ can (102 g)	42 g (1½ oz)	7 g (¼ oz)	4 meals daily
12 weeks	½ can (205 g)	84 g (3 oz)	9 g (⅓ oz)	3 meals daily
24 weeks	1 can (411 g)	168 g (6 oz)	14 g (½ oz)	2 meals daily

Typical diet sheet for a young German Shepherd Dog. Note that these are not absolute figures, and may well need to be modified in individual cases, depending on the dog, its environment and the brand of food used. Sufficient milk and water should be poured over the biscuit meal to soften it, especially for younger dogs, and fresh drinking water *must* always be available. Special tinned foods for puppies are now produced, and these should be used if possible.

Veterinary Considerations

The hind dew claws, if present, must be removed when the pups are about four days old. This gives the vet an opportunity to inspect the litter. If any have died, this is a cause for concern, as the 'Fading Puppy' syndrome may be implicated, and losses should be mentioned to the vet. Worming tablets and vaccinations, when the puppies are older, will also be required, and necessitate a further consultation.

6. Exhibiting and the Standard of the Breed

Showing a German Shepherd Dog, as with other breeds, affords an obvious opportunity both to see and compete against fellow dogs, which, for serious breeders, is an invaluable means of getting their bloodlines recognized. It also enables people of similar interests to meet, and probably develop friendships which will last for many years. This important side of exhibiting can sometimes be overlooked in the frenzy of the showring, but is as equally significant as winning.

Exhibition Management

There is no short-cut to regular successes where breeding, training and condition are all significant. A dog which compares very favorably with the Standard must, at the same time, be physically fit. This necessitates correct feeding and adequate exercise.

German Shepherd Dogs are, perhaps, more straightforward to prepare for a show than are many breeds. Their coat does not require any trimming, but thorough grooming on a daily basis is essential. Bathing is rarely required, and may actually remove some of the natural lustre from the coat, which would be detrimental. Therefore, if any mud gets on to the coat, it is preferable to allow the deposit to dry and harden, after which it can be brushed out.

Training is also an important feature of a good show dog, as is temperament. It must be used to having its mouth opened by strangers so that the teeth can be inspected by the judge. Prior to a show, these can be cleaned using a canine tooth paste, applied on damp cotton-wool. The dog will need to master the correct stance, with one hind leg positioned slightly backwards, while remaining evenly balanced on all limbs. It must also learn to remain still whilst being evaluated by the judge.

Good movement in the ring is the feature of a quality German Shepherd which has been taught to extend its legs to the maximum possible without actually running. The ideal is a dog which could carry a glassful of water on its back, during this motion, without any fluid actually being spilled. This requires good conformation of both fore and hind limbs, linked by a solid backbone, and is referred to as 'angulation'.

A chance to relax between classes at a dog show. Very much family affairs this young man is clearly enjoying his day out.

Show Entry

Exhibitors can only show dogs registered in their own names, so that, prior to entry, a transfer must be arranged through the Kennel Club, if necessary. It is also important to know if the dog has won any previous awards, which might restrict its entry to some classes. It is forbidden to exhibit any dog which, within the previous fortnight, has been vaccinated against distemper.

The show schedule for an event should be obtained as soon as possible, prior the show, and read carefully before completion. Shows fall into various categories of which the Championships are the most significant and highly contested. In the UK, the dog and bitch adjudged top of their breed are each awarded Challenge Certificates at these events. When a German Shepherd Dog achieves three of these certificates, awarded by different judges, it is a breed Champion. Under American rules, a Champion will have acquired fifteen points, with some major point wins of between three and five points, at shows with various judges.

The Standard of the Breed

There are three main breed standards in the German Shepherd, these being the German, the American and the British. The latter two were based on the original SV standard of 1899 but have, as has the German, been updated on numerous occasions. The limitations of this book do not permit the reproduction of all three standards; therefore it was decided to quote the American on the grounds that it is more detailed and covers items, such as number of teeth, which are not mentioned in either of the other two. The reader is advised to obtain a copy of the standard applicable to their country.

The American Standard
Reproduced by kind permission of the American Kennel Club

General Appearance

The first impression of a good German Shepherd Dog is that of a strong, agile, well-muscled animal, alert and full of life. It is well balanced, with harmonious development of the forequarter and hindquarter. The dog is longer than tall, deep-bodied, and presents an outline of smooth curves rather than angles. It looks substantial and not spindly, giving the impression, both at rest and in motion, of muscular fitness and nimbleness without any look of clumsiness or soft living. The ideal dog is stamped with a look of quality and nobility – difficult to define, but unmistakable when present. Secondary sex characteristics are strongly marked, and every animal gives a definite impression of masculinity or femininity, according to its sex.

Character

The breed has a distinct personality marked by direct and fearless, but not hostile, expression, self-confidence and a certain aloofness that does not lend itself to immediate and indiscriminate friendships. The dog must be approachable, quietly standing its ground and showing confidence and willingness to meet overtures without itself making them. It is poised, but when the occasion demands, eager and alert; both fit and willing to serve in its capacity as companion, watchdog, blind leader, herding dog, or guardian, whichever the circumstances may demand. The dog must not be timid, shrinking behind its master or handler; it should not be nervous, looking about or upward with anxious expression or showing nervous reactions, such as tucking of tail, to strange sounds or sights. Lack of confidence under any surroundings is not typical of good character. Any of the above deficiencies in character which indicate shyness must be penalized as very serious faults. It must be possible for the judge to observe the teeth and to determine that both testicles are descended. Any dog that attempts to bite the judge must be disqualified. The ideal dog is a working animal with an incorruptible character combined with body and gait suitable for the arduous work that constitutes its primary purpose.

This excellent study typifies the natural beauty of the German Shepherd Dog.

Head

The head is noble, cleanly chiseled, strong without coarseness, but above all not fine, and in proportion to the body. The head of the male is distinctively masculine, and that of the female distinctly feminine. The muzzle is long and strong with the lips firmly fitted, and its topline is parallel to the topline of the skull. Seen from the front, the forehead is only moderately arched, and the skull slopes into the long, wedge-shaped muzzle without abrupt stop. Jaws are strongly developed. *Ears* – Ears are moderately pointed, in proportion to the skull, open toward the front, and carried erect when at attention, the ideal carriage being one in which the centre lines of the ears, viewed from the front, are parallel to each other and perpendicular to the ground. A dog with cropped or hanging ears must be disqualified. *Eyes* – Of medium size, almond shaped, set a little obliquely and not protruding. The color is as dark as possible. The expression keen, intelligent and composed. *Teeth* – 42 in number – 20 upper and 22 lower – are strongly developed and meet in a scissors bite in which part of the inner surface of the upper incisors meet and engage part of the outer surface of the lower incisors. An overshot jaw or a level bite is undesirable. An undershot jaw is a disqualifying fault. Complete dentition is to be preferred. Any missing teeth other than first premolars is a serious fault.

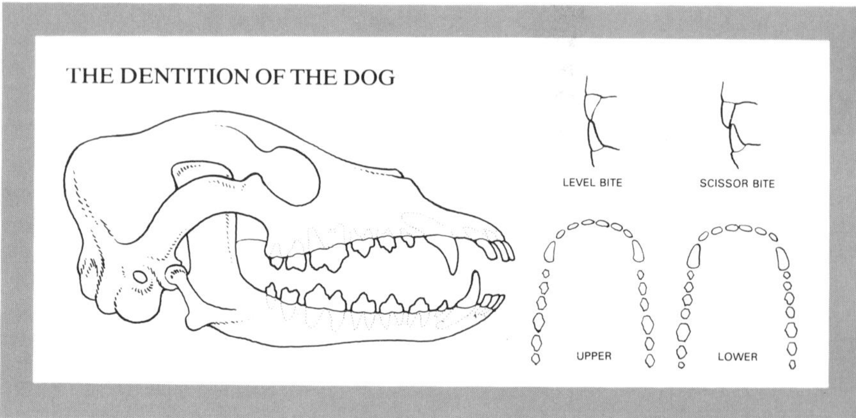

The dental formula for a mature German Shepherd should be:

$$2 \left(I \frac{3}{3} \; C \frac{1}{1} \; P \frac{4}{4} \; M \frac{2}{3} \right).$$

The incisors (I) are the teeth at the front of the mouth, with the pointed canines (C) behind them. The pre-molars (P) follow, and then the true molars (M), both of which have predominantly grinding surfaces. Using the recognized shorthand above, the upper figure gives the number of teeth which should be present in the top jaw, whereas the lower figures are for the corresponding teeth in the bottom jaw. The brackets, with the figure 2 in front, simply indicate that this is for one side of the face only, and so needs to be multiplied by two to obtain the total number of a particular type of tooth, or the overall total present in the mouth.

The pre-molars are most consistently decreased in number, and this is considered a serious breed fault, which is inherited. Under American rules, preference is given to German Shepherds with all their teeth present, while in Germany itself, dogs with missing teeth are penalized or even excluded from the SV Studbook.

32

Neck

The neck is strong and muscular, clean-cut and relatively long, proportionate in size to the head and without loose folds of skin. When the dog is at attention or excited, the head is raised and the neck carried high; otherwise typical carriage of the head is forward rather than up and but little higher than the top of the shoulders, particularly in motion.

Forequarters

The shoulder blades are long and obliquely angled, laid on flat and not placed forward. The upper arm joins the shoulder blade at about a right angle. Both the upper arm and the shoulder blade are well muscled. The forelegs, viewed from all sides, are straight and the bone oval rather than round. The pasterns are strong and springy and angulated at approximately a 25-degree angle from the vertical.

Feet

The feet are short, compact, with toes well arched, pads thick and firm, nails short and dark. The dewclaws, if any, should be removed from the hind legs. Dew-claws on the forelegs may be removed, but are normally left on.

Proportion

The German Shepherd Dog is longer than tall, with the most desirable proportion as 10 to 8½. The desired height for males at the top of the highest point of the shoulder blade is 24 to 26 inches; and for bitches, 22 to 24 inches. The length is measured from the point of the prosternum or breast bone to the rear edge of the pelvis, the ischial tuberosity. *(UK height equivalent: Dogs 61–66 cm. Bitches 55·8–61 cm.)*

Body

The whole structure of the body gives an impression of depth and solidity without bulkiness. *Chest* – Commencing at the prosternum, it is well filled and carried well down between the legs. It is deep and capacious, never shallow, with ample room for lungs and heart, carried well forward, and the prosternum showing ahead of the shoulder in profile. *Ribs* – Well sprung and long, neither barrel-shaped nor too flat, and carried down to a sternum which reaches to the elbows. Correct ribbing allows the elbows to move back freely when the dog is at a trot. Too round causes interference and throws the elbows out: too flat or short causes pinched elbows. Ribbing is carried well back so that the loin is relatively short. *Abdomen* – Firmly held and not paunchy. The bottom line is only moderately tucked up in the loin.

Topline

Withers – The withers are higher than and sloping into the level back. *Back* – The back is straight, very strongly developed without sag or roach, and relatively short. The desirable long proportion is not derived from a long back, but from over-all length with relation to height, which is achieved by length of forequarter and length of withers and hindquarter, viewed from the side. *Loin* – Viewed from the top, broad and strong. Undue length between the last rib and the thigh, when viewed from the side, is undesirable. *Croup* – Long and gradually sloping. *Tail* – Bushy, with the last vertebra extended at least to the hock joint. It is set smoothly into the croup and low rather than high. At rest, the tail hangs in a slight curve like a sabre. A slight hook – sometimes carried to one side – is faulty only to the extent that it mars general appearance. When the dog is excited or in motion, the curve is accentuated and the tail is raised, but it should never be curled forward beyond a vertical line. Tails too short, or with clumpy ends due to ankylosis, are serious faults. A dog with a docked tail must be disqualified.

Hindquarters

The whole assembly of the thigh, viewed from the side is broad, with both upper and lower thigh well muscled, forming as nearly as possible a right angle. The upper thigh bone parallels the shoulder blade while the lower thigh bone parallels the upper arm. The metatarsus (the unit between the hock joint and the foot) is short, strong and tightly articulated.

Gait

A German Shepherd Dog is a trotting dog, and its structure has been developed to meet the requirements of its work. *General Impression* – The gait is outreaching, elastic, seemingly without effort, smooth and rhythmic, covering the maximum amount of ground with the minimum number of steps. At a walk it covers a great deal of ground with long stride of both hind legs and forelegs. At a trot the dog covers still more ground with even longer stride, and moves powerfully but easily, with co-ordination and balance so that the gait appears to be the steady motion of a well-lubricated machine. The feet travel close to the ground on both forward reach and backward push. In order to achieve ideal movement of this kind, there must be good

A superb study of a saddle-marked black and tan German Shepherd Dog.

A young girl proudly 'sets up' her Shepherd for this photograph.

muscular development and ligamentation. The hindquarters deliver, through the back, a powerful forward thrust which slightly lifts the whole animal and drives the body forward. Reaching far under, and passing the imprint left by the front foot, the hind foot takes hold of the ground; then hock, stifle and upper thigh come into play and sweep back, the stroke of the hind leg finishing with the foot still close to the ground in a smooth follow-through. The overreach of the hindquarter usually necessitates one hind foot passing outside and the other hind foot passing inside the track of the forefeet, and such action is not faulty unless the locomotion is crabwise with the dog's body sideways out of the normal straight line.

Transmission

The typical smooth, flowing gait is maintained with great strength and firmness of back. The whole effort of the hindquarters is transmitted to the forequarter through the loin, back and withers. At full trot, the back must remain firm and level without sway, roll, whip or roach. Unlevel topline with withers lower than the hip is a fault. To compensate for the forward motion imparted by the hindquarters, the shoulder should open to its full extent. The forelegs should reach out close to the ground in a long stride in harmony with that of the hindquarters. The dog does not track on widely separated parallel lines, but brings the feet inward toward the middle line of the body when trotting in order to maintain balance. The feet track closely but do not strike or cross over. Viewed from the front, the front legs function from the shoulder joint to the pad in a straight line. Viewed from the rear, the hind legs function from the hip joint to the pad in a straight line. Faults of gait, whether from front, rear or side, are to be considered very serious faults.

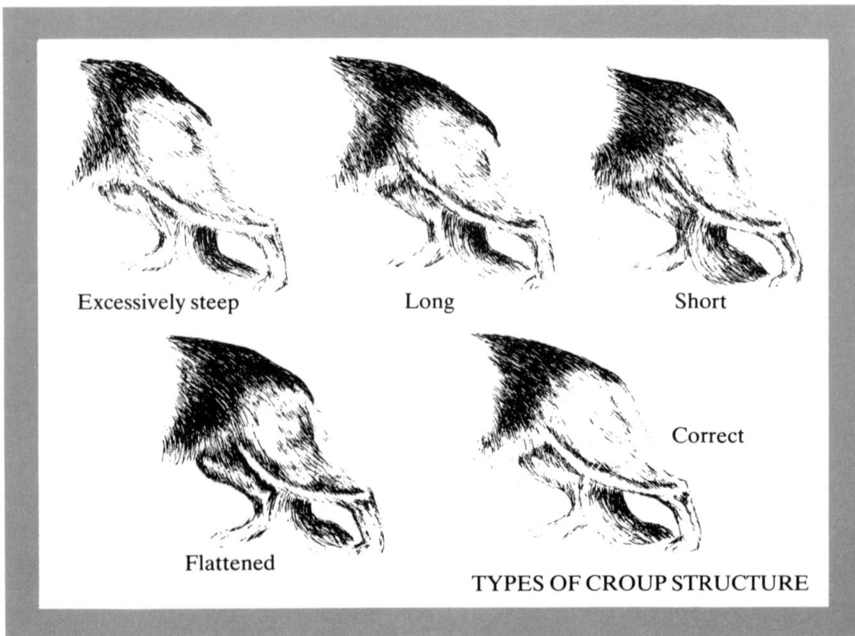

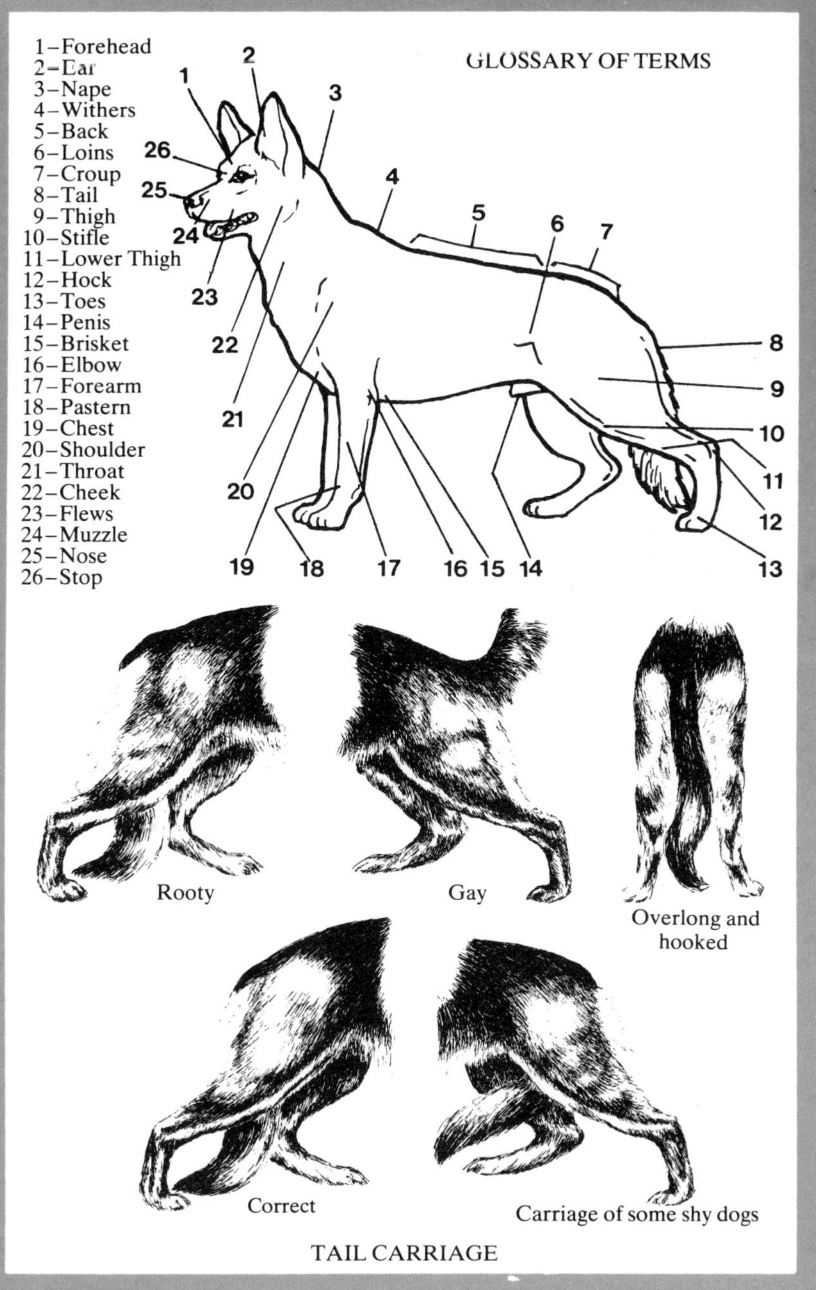

Rooty

Gay

Overlong and hooked

Correct

Carriage of some shy dogs

TAIL CARRIAGE

A fine pair of German
Shepherd Dogs relax at
a show.

Color

The German Shepherd Dog varies in color, and most colors are permissible. Strong rich colors are preferred. Nose black, Pale, washed-out colors and blues or livers are serious faults. A white dog or a dog with a nose that is not predominantly black, must be disqualified.

Coat

The ideal dog has a double coat of medium length. The outer coat should be as dense as possible, hair straight, harsh and lying close to the body. A slightly wavy outer coat, often of wiry texture, is permissible. The head, including the inner ear and fore-face, and the legs and paws are covered with short hair, and the neck with longer and thicker hair. The rear of the forelegs and hind legs has somewhat longer hair extending to the pastern and hock, respectively. Faults in coat include, soft, silky, too long outer coat, woolly, curly, and open coat.

Disqualifications
Cropped or hanging ears.
Undershot jaw.
Docked tail.
White dogs.
Dogs with noses not predominantly black.
Any dog that attempts to bite the judge.

7. Health and Disease

This chapter is not intended to act as a replacement for veterinary advice, which should always be sought when a dog appears poorly. In Britain, only vets are allowed to diagnose and treat ailments. They can prescribe antibiotics and other modern drugs, to maximize the chances of a successful recovery. In addition, with the advent of effective vaccines, diseases such as distemper, which were formerly common killers, are now rarely encountered. Even canine parvovirus, a new disease which has suddenly appeared worldwide during the last few years, is now controlled efficiently by vaccination. Nevertheless, dogs must still be vaccinated (and given boosters as necessary) because, if they otherwise encounter the infection, they are as likely to succumb as their predecessors, without the vaccine's protection.

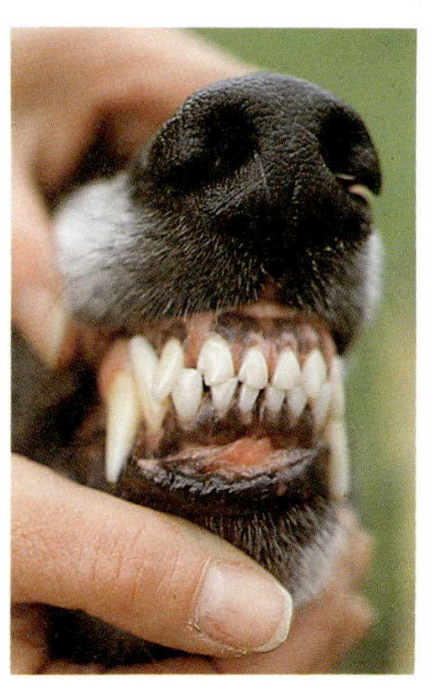

Inspection of the teeth should be made to look for signs of decay.

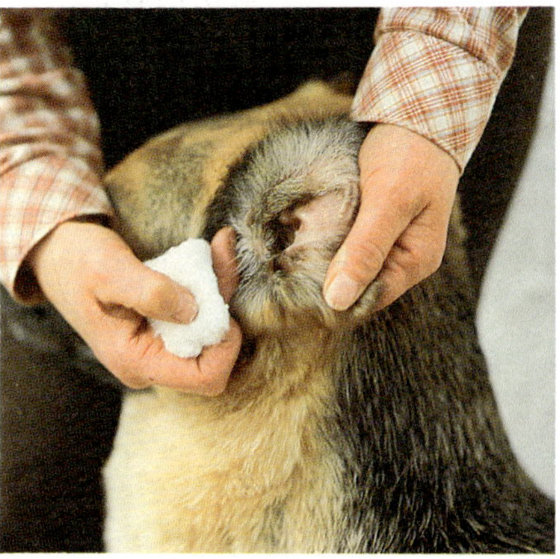

Thankfully, GSDs have few ear problems – a regular check and clean is usually all that is needed.

Bleeding

Applying pressure to the site which is bleeding, using a wet cotton wool pad, is an effective means of stemming even severe blood loss. Minor wounds will respond to being bathed with a solution of potash alum, or even a styptic pencil. If there is a risk of infection, espcially with a deep wound, a vet should be consulted.

Claws

These may need to be cut back on occasions, especially if the dog has no access to hard surfaces. The claws must always be checked prior to a show, in case their length affects the dog's gait. It is not easy to spot the 'quick' or blood supply of the claws and, as they are very tough, the vet should be visited for this task to be carried out.

Coughing

There are various causes of this complaint. 'Kennel cough' is regrettably common in dogs, usually after they have come out of kennels. There is now a vaccine against one of the main bacteria, *Bordetella bronchoseptica*, causing the infection. It is not generally a serious problem, but another possible cause of coughing, a bone stuck in the throat may require urgent veterinary attention.

Diarrhoea

Diarrhoea is again a symptom of a disease, rather than a disease itself. Various infections may be implicated as the cause. In the case of parvovirus infection, the faeces are often blood-stained. The accompanying loss of fluid will soon result in severe circulatory disorders if left untreated.

A possible non-infective cause of diarrhoea in German Shepherd Dogs, which appear healthy and eat well, yet lose weight over a period of time, is a pancreatic insufficiency. The enzymes produced by the pancreas to digest the food properly are deficient but once the condition has been confirmed by tests on the faeces, there are various commercial preparations available which will counter this. The addition of approximately 115 gms (4 oz) of ox pancreas ('Sweetbreads') to each meal can also be a useful supplement.

Epilepsy

This neurological disorder is a distressing condition, but treatments are available to combat the risk of convulsions. These may last a couple of minutes or even less, with the dog becoming prostrate, and paddling on its side. It will usually lose control of both bladder and bowel functions during such episodes. Afterwards, recovery may be quite rapid, but the dog should be kept quiet. As epilepsy appears to have a hereditary basis in the German Shepherd, affected dogs should not be used for breeding purposes.

Fleas

These parasites are a common problem, especially during the warmer months of the year. They feed on the dog's blood causing irritation and bouts of scratching and may lead to an allergic reaction against the flea's saliva. It is possible to detect them in the fur by means of a fine metal flea comb, sold by many pet stores. Adult fleas, or more commonly their dirt visible as black specks, can be seen when the comb with its load of hair is examined against a white background. Any fleas should be put in water immediately, or 'popped' firmly between the fingernails to prevent them hopping off.

Treatments obtained from a vet may be in the form of a powder, aerosol spray or a wash which, although effective, will necessitate repeated use; flea collars and medallions are effective over a much longer period. They must be used as directed to prevent unpleasant side effects.

Fleas also live in the dog's immediate surroundings so that its sleeping quarters must be treated, to prevent re-infection. Cats, as well as hedgehogs, can spread fleas to dogs, but if a cat is also found to be infected, care should be taken over the preparation used, because not all are safe for use on felines.

Hip Dysplasia

The German Shepherd, like other large breeds, can suffer from this complaint. The hip joint is effectively a ball and socket structure, with the head of the femur normally fitting snugly into the cup of the acetabulum on the hip. Various factors, such as an abnormally shallow acetabulum will affect this structural arrangement and serve to weaken the joint.

Although pups may appear normal at birth, symptoms can become evident as early as five months later, and are usually manifested by pain in the affected joints. The hips themselves are not fully developed at this stage, with areas of cartilage still to be replaced by bone, so a variable degree of malformation may occur. Indeed, not all dogs are affected as severely as others.

Various schemes are now operating to detect cases of hip dysplasia, prior to breeding, as the problem can be inherited. It is diagnosed by radiography, preferably between two and two-and-a-half years of age. Positioning of the legs is crucial in obtaining a reliable X-ray picture, so some form of anaesthetic may be required. Breeding from stock showing this complaint should not, of course, be undertaken. In the UK the German Shepherd Dog Improvement Foundation was formed to monitor this type of problem.

Rabies

This dreaded viral disease can affect all mammals and not just dogs, although, if infected, they, by virtue of their close contact, then represent a considerable hazard to human health. The virus is endemic in the fox population of parts of Europe and also in the wildlife of areas of North America.

Rabies is not at present found in Britain or Australia, and there are strict quarantine regulations to ensure that the infection does not gain access to these countries. Information about the movement of dogs, as well as semen for artificial insemination purposes, should be addressed to the appropriate agricultural department of the country concerned, well in advance of the proposed date of import or export.

Worms

The common types of worms encountered in dogs, especially young animals, are roundworms and tapeworms. The roundworm species *Toxocara canis* is potentially one of the most serious, because it can infect children, and may cause blindness. Thankfully, such occurrences are rare.

Infection passes from the bitch to her developing puppies, which are born with the worms in their intestines. They should, therefore, be treated from the age of a fortnight, along with the bitch. At this stage, the worms will not have matured sufficiently to produce eggs, so the hazard of human infection will be much lessened if they are eliminated before they can reproduce. Cleanliness is essential, as the eggs will survive in dirty surroundings. As additional precautions, the wearing of gloves when cleaning up and supervizing contact between children and puppies, as well as thorough hand-washing afterwards, are to be recommended.

Fleas act as intermediate hosts for one of the most common genera of tapeworm, *Dipylidium*, and so control of both parasites is required to break the cycle of this infection. Dogs can also become infected from eating the flesh of herbivores which contain intermediate stages of the tapeworm. Treatment, as for roundworms, is by means of a worming dose given in tablet form. Extremely effective remedies are now available from veterinarians.

In some parts of the world, including parts of America and Australia, heartworms are a significant threat to a dog's health. These can live for years in the right ventricle of the heart and adjacent regions of the circulatory system. The intermediate stages, known as microfilariae, are transmitted from one dog to another by insects such as mosquitoes. It is a very difficult infection to treat, but can be prevented by giving appropriate medication.

A magnificent study to end this book – three generations of German Shepherd Dogs.

My Dog's Information Page

Kennel Club Name: _______________________________________

No. __________ ____

Pet Name: _________________________________ Sex: _________

Color: _____________________________ Date of Birth: _________

Sire: ____

Dam: ____

Breeder: ____

____

Date Purchased: ____________________ Identity No. _________

Vaccinations Given: _______________________________________

Date: _____________________ Boosters Due: _______________

Useful Telephone Numbers

Breeder: ___________________ Veterinarian: _______________

Boarding Kennel: _____________ Kennel Club: _____________

Training Class: ________________ Pet Store: _______________

Police/Dog Pound: ____

Glossary of German Terms

When consulting pedigrees, confusion may arise over the use of German terms. These, with abbreviations and corresponding English meanings, are given below in alphabetical order.

Abzeichen (A): Markings
Ahnen: Ancestors
Ahnentafel: Pedigree
Allgemeine Erscheinung: General appearance
Alter: Age
Alterklasse (A.K.): Adult class
Angekört: Dog has undergone a breed survey
Augen: Eyes
Befriedigend (B): Fair
Behaarung: Coat
Belegt: Bred
Besitzer: Owner
Bewertung: Qualification
Breit: Broad
Deckfarbe: Main color
Drahthaarig: Wire-coated
Enkel/Enkelin: Grandson/ granddaughter
Fang: Muzzle
Farbe: Color
Fassbeinig: Bow-legged
Gang: Gait
Gelb (g): Tan, gold
Gesundheit: Health
Geworfen: Whelped
Glatthaarig: Smooth-coated
Grosseltern: Grandparents
Guter Zustand: Fine condition
Hacken: Hocks
Höhe: Height
Jugendklasse (J.K.L.): Youth class
Körbuch: Register of breed-surveyed dogs

Kurz: Short
Langhaarig: Long-coated
Läufe: Legs
Mangelhaft: Faulty
Mutter: Dam
Pfote: Paw
Rasse: Breed
Rein: Pure
Rude (R): Male dog
Schussgleichgültig: Gun-shy
Sieger (S): Champion dog
Stockhaar: Normal coat
Traben: Trot
Überbeiss: Overshot
Überwinkelt: Over-angulated
Vater: Sire
Verein: Club
Vorbeiss: Undershot
Vorschub: Length (of gait)
Vorzüglich: Excellent
Wesen: Temperament
Wesenscheu: Shyness
Zuchtbuchnummer: Stud book number
Zuchtprüfung: Approved for breeding

The German Shepherd at a Glance

Country of Origin	Germany
First Established as a Breed	1899
KC Grouping	Working
Synonyms	Alsatian, Alsatian Wolf Dog
Uses	Tracking, Guards, Sentry Dogs, Rescue, Drug Detection, Guide Dogs, Police Work, Shepherding, Companions
Height: Male Female	61–66 cm (24–26 in) 55·8–61 cm (22–24 in)
Weight	This is not specifically given in either the UK, USA or German Standards but, as a guide, dogs will be approx. 34–39 kg (75–85 lbs) and bitches 27–36 kg (60–80 lbs)
Length to Height Ratio	10:9 and 10:8·5
Normal Rectal Temp.	38·6°C (101·5°F)
Number of Teeth	42 (Adult), 28 (Puppy Milk Teeth)
Number of Chromosomes	78
Breeding Season	Twice annually
Duration of Oestrus	21 days
Gestation Period	63 days (9 weeks). Period between fertilization of egg and parturition (puppy birth)
Average Litter Size	7–8
Puppies' Eyes Open	Approx. 12th day or soon after
Longevity (average)	9·6 years (Male), 10·1 (Female) (Willis 1976)

Food Weight Requirement:
  Puppy
 	
  Adult
	At 8 weeks old ½ kg (1 lb) min. per day, plus meal
	Tinned 822 gms (29 ozs),
	Fresh meat 1 kg (2 lbs), plus meal

Coat Color	Black, tan, gold, silver in combination or pure black. Undesirable: white

Bibliography

Ash, E. C.	1936	*The Alsatian*, Cassell, London, 154pp
Brockwell, D.	—	*The Alsatian*, Hutchinson, London, 241pp
Bennett, J. G.	1982	**The Complete German Shepherd*, Howell, New York, 352pp
Denlinger, M. G.	1947	*The Complete German Shepherd*, Denlinger, Washington D.C., 256pp
Elliott, N.	1961	**The Complete Alsatian*, Nicholas Vane, London, 288pp
	1968	*Modern Bloodlines In The Alsatian*, Nicholas Vane, London
Goldbecker, W. & Hart, E.	1960	**This Is The German Shepherd*, T.F.H., Neptune, N.J., 253pp
Horowitz, G.	1923	*The Alsatian Wolf Dog*, Our Dogs, Manchester, 79pp
Humphrey, E. & Warner, L. H.	1934	**Working Dogs; An Attempt To Produce A Strain Of German Shepherds*, Johns Hopkins University Press, Baltimore, 256pp
Leonard, L.	1956	*Alsatians*, W. & G. Foyle, London, 95pp
Pickett, F. N.	1950	*The Book Of The Alsatian Dog*, Weald Press, London, 176pp
Pickup, M.	1964	*The Alsatian Owners Encyclopaedia*, Pelham, London, 104pp
	1969	*German Shepherd Guide*, Pet Library, New York, 250pp
	1973	*All About The German Shepherd*, Pelham, London
Schwabacher, J.	1922	*The Popular Alsatian*, Popular Dogs, London, 82pp
Schwabacher, J. & Gray, T.	1967	*The Alsatian (German Shepherd Dog)*, Popular Dogs, London, 254pp
Stephanitz, M. von	1923	*The German Shepherd Dog In Word And Picture*, Anton Kampfe, Jena
	1950	**8th Edition*, Verein für Deutsche Schäferhunde, Augsburg, 983pp
Tidbold, M.	1978	*The German Shepherd Dog: Its Care and Training*, K & R Books, Edlington, Lincs, 102pp

continued overleaf

Bibliography *continued*

Willis   1976 *The German Shepherd Dog: Its History, Development and Genetics*, K & R Books, Edlington, Lincs.

A number of the above books are now out of print and may be difficult to locate. Those marked * are especially recommended.

Kennel Club addresses

American Kennel Club,
51 Madison Avenue,
New York,
N.Y.10010.

Australian Kennel Club,
Royal Show Grounds,
Ascot Vale,
Victoria,
Australia.

British Kennel Club,
1 Clarges Street,
Piccadilly,
London W.1.

Canadian Kennel Club,
2150 Bloor Street West,
Toronto M6S 1M8,
Ontario.

Irish Kennel Club,
23 Earlsfort Terrace,
Dublin 2.

Kennel Union of Southern Africa,
6th Floor, Bree Castle,
68 Bree Street,
Cape Town 8001.

Malaysian Kennel Association,
PO Box 559,
Kuala Lumpur,
Malaya.

New Zealand Kennel Club,
PO Box 19,
101 Aro Street,
Wellington.

The Singapore Kennel Club,
275f Selegie Complex,
Selegie Road,
Singapore 7.